D0881043

GRAPHIC FORENSIC SCIENCE
CRIME SCENE INVESTIGATORS

by Rob Shone

illustrated by Claudia Saraceni

rosen publishing's
rosen
central®

New York

Published in 2008 by The Rosen Publishing Group, Inc.
29 East 21st Street, New York, NY 10010

First edition, 2008

Designed and produced by
David West Books

Editor: Gail Bushnell

Photo credits:
P4, istockphoto.com/Stephen Sweet; 6t, NCIS; 6b, Department of Defense; 7m(both), Stechondanet; 7b, istockphoto.com/James Ferrie; 44t, Bob Adams; 44b, istockphoto.com/Stephan Klein; 45t, istockphoto.com/Stephan Klein.

Library of Congress Cataloging-in-Publication Data

Shone, Rob.
  Crime scene investigators / Rob Shone ; illustrated by Claudia
Saraceni. -- 1st ed.
      p. cm. -- (Graphic forensic science)
  Includes index.
  ISBN 978-1-4042-1443-9 (library binding) -- ISBN 978-1-4042-1444-6
(pbk.) -- ISBN 978-1-4042-1445-3 (6 pack)
  1. Criminal investigation--United States--Case studies. 2. Crime
scenes--United States--Case studies. 3. Crime scene searches--United
States--Case studies. I. Title.
  HV8073.S436 2008
  363.25'2--dc22
                                          2007043389

Manufactured in China

CONTENTS

SOLVING A MURDER

Police investigating crimes today, especially murders, are relying more and more on science to help solve those crimes.

THE BODY OF EVIDENCE

When a crime has been discovered, crime scene investigators are called in to protect the crime scene from being spoiled, and to gather evidence. This evidence is looked at in detail by experts called forensic scientists. In many cases the evidence has not only helped the police catch the criminals but has also been vital in convicting them in court.

All evidence has to be bagged and tagged carefully, since it may be used later in court.

THE CRIME SCENE
The first on the crime scene are usually the police. A detective (1) is put in charge of the case. CSI–Crime Scene Investigators (2) are sent for, and an ME–Medical Examiner or Coroner (3) is informed. The ME may well visit the crime scene to examine the body, and is in charge of the crime scene evidence. The CSI team carries out a detailed examination of the scene, gathering evidence as well as making a record of the scene with photographs, sketches, and notes.

THE CRIME LAB
The evidence (A) is taken to a crime laboratory, where it is looked at, in detail, by forensic scientists (4). These are experts in fields such as ballistics (guns and bullets), trace evidence such as DNA, fingerprinting, pathology (examining dead bodies for evidence), toolmarks (evidence of weapons), entomology (insect life), and criminal profiling (criminal behavior), to name just a few. Certain forensic scientists may also visit the crime scene to gather evidence. Various pieces of evidence, such as footwear prints, fingerprints, and DNA, are entered into archives (B).

ARCHIVES
These archives are also used to match evidence, such as fingerprints, found at the crime scene.
Finally, a report based on the evidence is given to the police to help catch and convict the killer (C).

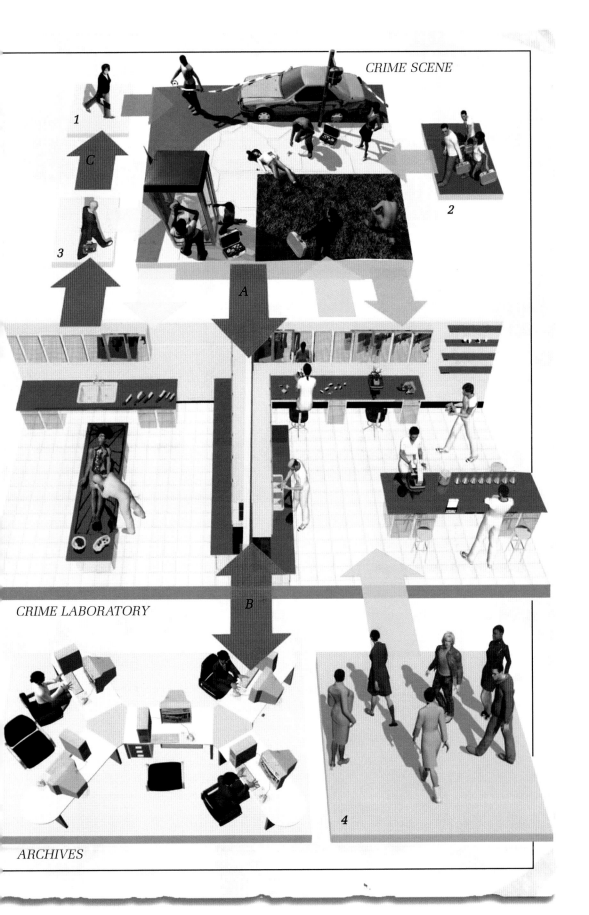

CRIME SCENE

1

C

3

2

A

CRIME LABORATORY

B

ARCHIVES

4

THE CRIME SCENE

Crime scenes come in all shapes and sizes. To a CSI team each one is a challenge.

FIRST IMPRESSIONS

Once the investigators have decided on how big the crime scene is, they make its boundaries secure. Unauthorized people are kept away so they don't damage crucial evidence. The investigators then carry out a walk-through of the scene. The CSI officers move slowly through the scene on a set path, making notes as they go along. They look for anything that seems out of place. They also decide if they need any special equipment or the services of an expert such as a forensic entomologist.

Some military forces have their own crime scene investigators. Here, an NCIS (Naval Criminal Investigative Service) team carries out an exercise on board the aircraft carrier USS Wright.

When 9/11 happened it turned the Twin Towers into a disaster area, and created a massive crime scene.

RECORDING THE SCENE

A second walk-through follows the first. This time the CSI officer will begin to document the scene. The officer will take notes and photographs of the scene. Other photographs are taken showing the whole scene. Sometimes onlooking members of the public are photographed. One may well be the culprit.

SEARCHING THE SCENE

Now a thorough search of the crime scene can begin. There are several patterns the search can take. Starting at the center of the scene, an officer might work outward in a spiral shape. For larger areas the entire CSI team might move in a line across the scene. Other methods include the zonal search, where the scene is split up into sections.

Sherlock Holmes, the fictional detective, solved crimes by coming to logical conclusions deduced from the evidence that he had found.

Evidence is photographed where it is found along with a ruler.

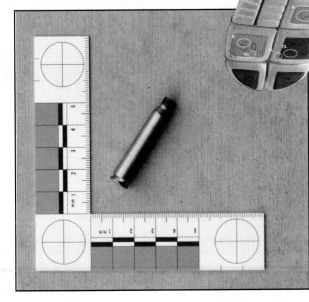

Once it has been collected, the evidence is processed and analyzed. Here a footprint has been matched to the shoe that made it.

COLLECTING THE EVIDENCE

Great care is taken when collecting evidence. If it becomes tainted it might be useless in a court case. Each item, if it can fit, is sealed in a plastic evidence bag and logged. Generally, a CSI officer's involvement in a crime scene ends after this stage. The evidence is sent to the crime lab and the technicians take over.

THE MORMON FORGERY MURDERS

TUESDAY, OCTOBER 15, 1985. EVEN THOUGH IT WAS 6:45 A.M. AND WOULD NOT BE LIGHT FOR ANOTHER HOUR, THERE WAS ACTIVITY INSIDE SALT LAKE CITY'S COURTHOUSE.

Steven Christensen

THE BOMB HAD EXPLODED AT A HOUSE IN HOLLADAY, A SUBURB OF SALT LAKE CITY. A WOMAN LAY DEAD IN THE DRIVEWAY.

HER NAME'S KATHLEEN SHEETS—A NEIGHBOR IDENTIFIED HER. WITNESSES SAY THAT THE BOMB WENT OFF AT AROUND 9:30. THEY FOUND HER BODY AN HOUR LATER.

THEY FOUND THIS SCRAP OF PAPER FROM THE BOMB'S WRAPPING. IT SEEMS IT WAS ADDRESSED TO GARY SHEETS, KATHLEEN'S HUSBAND.

LET'S FIND OUT IF THERE'S A CONNECTION BETWEEN SHEETS AND CHRISTENSEN.

MEANWHILE, AT THE COURTHOUSE, CHRISTENSEN'S BODY HAD BEEN TAKEN AWAY. THE CRIME SCENE INVESTIGATORS COULD START THEIR WORK.

AN UNDAMAGED OFFICE HAD BEEN TURNED INTO A POLICE COMMAND CENTER.

HERE'S A PLAN OF THE HALLWAY AND CHRISTENSEN'S OFFICE. I'VE DIVIDED IT UP INTO A GRID. WE CAN MARK ON IT WHERE ANY EVIDENCE IS FOUND.

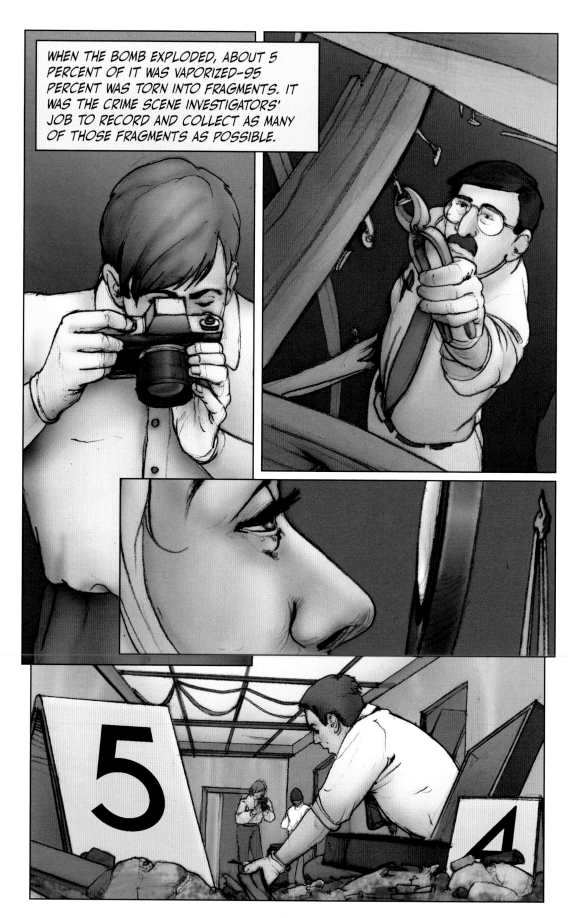

WHEN THE BOMB EXPLODED, ABOUT 5 PERCENT OF IT WAS VAPORIZED–95 PERCENT WAS TORN INTO FRAGMENTS. IT WAS THE CRIME SCENE INVESTIGATORS' JOB TO RECORD AND COLLECT AS MANY OF THOSE FRAGMENTS AS POSSIBLE.

VACUUM CLEANERS WERE USED TO COLLECT THE SMALLEST FRAGMENTS.

EVEN PIECES OF THE CARPET WERE TAKEN TO BE TESTED FOR EXPLOSIVE CHEMICALS.

FILES AND COMPUTERS WERE TAKEN AWAY.

WHEN THEY FINISHED, THEY HAD FOUND 164 PIECES OF THE BOMB.

MORE BOMB FRAGMENTS WERE COLLECTED AT THE MORGUE...

THE BLAST CRUSHED HIS CHEST. PARTS OF THE BOMB ARE STILL EMBEDDED IN IT. HERE'S A PIECE OF WIRE...

...AND I THINK THIS IS PART OF A BATTERY.

BUT THIS IS WHAT KILLED HIM.

IT WENT THROUGH THE EYE SOCKET AND INTO HIS BRAIN.

WHILE THE FORENSIC TEAM WORKED, THE POLICE WERE TRYING TO FIND A MOTIVE FOR THE MURDERS.

UNTIL RECENTLY CHRISTENSEN WORKED FOR GARY SHEETS.

SHEETS RUNS A FINANCE COMPANY, BUT IT HAS MONEY PROBLEMS.

THERE ARE PLENTY OF PEOPLE WHO INVESTED MONEY WITH THE COMPANY AND LOST IT. THEY MIGHT WANT REVENGE.

HERE'S A COMPUTER PRINTOUT WITH THE NAMES OF THREE THOUSAND PEOPLE ON IT, EVERY ONE OF THEM AN INVESTOR IN SHEETS'S COMPANY AND EVERY ONE OF THEM A SUSPECT.

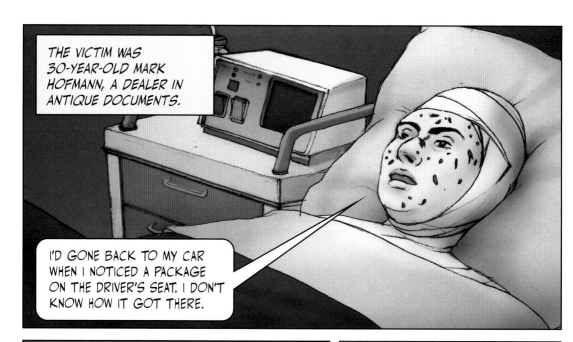

THE VICTIM WAS 30-YEAR-OLD MARK HOFMANN, A DEALER IN ANTIQUE DOCUMENTS.

I'D GONE BACK TO MY CAR WHEN I NOTICED A PACKAGE ON THE DRIVER'S SEAT. I DON'T KNOW HOW IT GOT THERE.

WHEN I OPENED THE CAR DOOR THE PACKAGE FELL ONTO THE FLOOR AND EXPLODED. I DON'T REMEMBER ANYTHING ELSE.

BOB SWEHLA HAD BEEN JOINED BY AGENT JERRY TAYLOR, A BOMB EXPERT FROM SAN FRANCISCO'S ATF OFFICE.

IT COULDN'T HAVE HAPPENED THE WAY HOFMANN SAID IT DID.

THERE SHOULD BE MARKS FROM THE EXPLOSION ON THE FLOOR OF THE CAR, BUT THERE AREN'T ANY.

THERE **ARE** MARKS ON THE CONSOLE BETWEEN THE SEATS. THAT'S WHERE THE BOMB EXPLODED.

THAT MAKES SENSE. A WITNESS SAYS SHE SAW HOFMANN REACHING BEHIND THE DRIVER'S SEAT FOR SOMETHING. HE WAS INSIDE THE CAR, NOT OUTSIDE, WHEN THE BOMB WENT OFF.

WHY WOULD HE LIE, THOUGH? I THINK WE SHOULD TAKE A CLOSER LOOK AT HIM.

THEY FOUND THAT HOFMANN AND CHRISTENSEN KNEW EACH OTHER. HOFMANN HAD UNCOVERED AND SOLD A NUMBER OF RARE AND IMPORTANT HISTORICAL DOCUMENTS TO THE MORMON CHURCH.

HOFMANN WAS TRYING TO SELL THE CHURCH A SET OF DOCUMENTS CALLED THE McCLELLIN COLLECTION. HE CLAIMED THEY SHED LIGHT ON THE FIRST MORMONS.

CHRISTENSEN WAS HELPING TO SEE THE DEAL THROUGH. HE WAS SUPPOSED TO HAVE MET WITH HOFMANN ON THE MORNING OF THE FIRST BOMB ATTACK.

HOFMANN WAS HAVING MONEY WORRIES AND NEEDED CHRISTENSEN TO COMPLETE THE McCLELLIN DEAL. HE DIDN'T KNOW GARY SHEETS, SO IT'S HARD TO SEE WHAT HIS MOTIVES WERE FOR EITHER MURDER.

I STILL CAN'T HELP THINKING HE'S INVOLVED SOMEHOW.

MEANWHILE, THE FORENSIC TEAM HAD BEEN EXAMINING THE BOMB FRAGMENTS.

ALL THREE WERE PIPE BOMBS AND MADE BY THE SAME PERSON, AGENT SWEHLA.

THE BOMBS LOOKED LIKE THIS.

"THE DETONATION CAUSED A HUGE EXPLOSION."

THE POLICE MANAGED TO GET A WARRANT TO SEARCH HOFMANN'S HOME.

REMEMBER, WE'RE LOOKING FOR ANYTHING CONNECTED WITH BOMBS OR BOMB-MAKING EQUIPMENT.

THE POLICE TOOK AWAY 5,000 PIECES OF EVIDENCE, INCLUDING...

A GREEN LETTER-JACKET— WITHOUT A LETTER!

THE EVIDENCE AGAINST HOFMANN WAS MOUNTING, BUT THE POLICE STILL DID NOT HAVE A MOTIVE. AT THE ATTORNEY GENERAL'S OFFICE DOCUMENT EXAMINER GEORGE THROCKMORTON WAS TAKING AN INTEREST IN THE STORY.

SOMETHING'S NOT RIGHT HERE. NO DEALER IS LUCKY ENOUGH TO FIND **THAT** MANY IMPORTANT DOCUMENTS.

THROCKMORTON WENT TO SEE A DOCUMENT DEALER HE KNEW AND ASKED TO BORROW DOCUMENTS THAT COULD BE TRACED BACK TO MARK HOFMANN.

THEY'VE ALL BEEN AUTHENTICATED BY EXPERTS. THE PAPER AND INK ARE THE RIGHT AGE, AND THE WRITING IS SMITH'S.

I HAVE THESE LETTERS WRITTEN BY JOSEPH SMITH.* THEY'RE DATED 1844. I DON'T SEE HOW THEY CAN BE FAKES, THOUGH.

*THE FOUNDER OF MORMONISM.

LATER...

THAT'S ODD. HERE ARE THREE LETTERS WRITTEN BY THE SAME PERSON ON THE SAME DAY AND IN THE SAME PLACE. YET I CAN SEE THAT THE PAPER, THE INK, AND THE PEN USED IS DIFFERENT IN EACH CASE.

THEY MUST HAVE BEEN FORGED AT DIFFERENT TIMES AND AUTHENTICATED BY THREE DIFFERENT DEALERS.

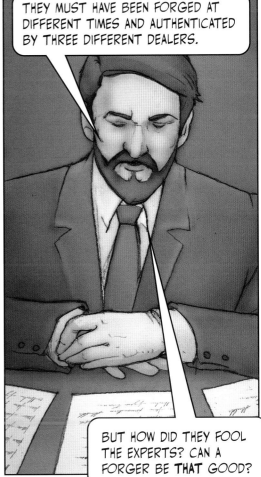

BUT HOW DID THEY FOOL THE EXPERTS? CAN A FORGER BE **THAT** GOOD?

THROCKMORTON WAS JOINED IN HIS INVESTIGATIONS BY DOCUMENT EXAMINER BILL FLYNN FROM PHOENIX, ARIZONA.

COPYING THE HANDWRITING AND GETTING HOLD OF OLD PAPER IS EASY. AGING THE INK TO MATCH—THAT'S THE HARD PART.

THIS MAY HELP—"GREAT FORGERS AND FAMOUS FAKES." IT WAS ONE OF THE THINGS THE POLICE TOOK FROM HOFMANN'S HOME.

AT LEAST WE MIGHT BE ABLE TO FIGURE OUT HOW HE **MADE** HIS INK.

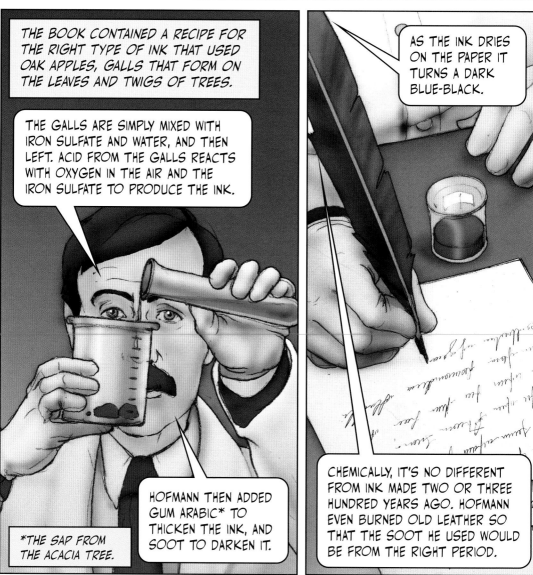

THE BOOK CONTAINED A RECIPE FOR THE RIGHT TYPE OF INK THAT USED OAK APPLES, GALLS THAT FORM ON THE LEAVES AND TWIGS OF TREES.

THE GALLS ARE SIMPLY MIXED WITH IRON SULFATE AND WATER, AND THEN LEFT. ACID FROM THE GALLS REACTS WITH OXYGEN IN THE AIR AND THE IRON SULFATE TO PRODUCE THE INK.

HOFMANN THEN ADDED GUM ARABIC* TO THICKEN THE INK, AND SOOT TO DARKEN IT.

*THE SAP FROM THE ACACIA TREE.

AS THE INK DRIES ON THE PAPER IT TURNS A DARK BLUE-BLACK.

CHEMICALLY, IT'S NO DIFFERENT FROM INK MADE TWO OR THREE HUNDRED YEARS AGO. HOFMANN EVEN BURNED OLD LEATHER SO THAT THE SOOT HE USED WOULD BE FROM THE RIGHT PERIOD.

FOR THE NEXT STEP, FLYNN AND THROCKMORTON MADE SAMPLE DOCUMENTS.

THEY THEN TRIED TO AGE THEM USING INFORMATION IN "GREAT FORGERS AND FAMOUS FAKES."

THEY FOUND THAT BATHING THE DOCUMENTS IN AMMONIA AND THEN HYDROGEN PEROXIDE, TWO TYPES OF BLEACH, WORKED THE BEST.

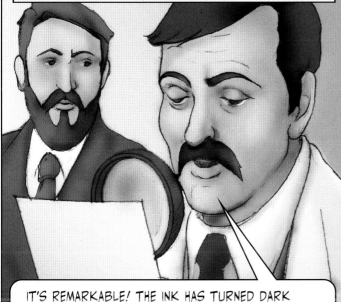

IT'S REMARKABLE! THE INK HAS TURNED DARK BROWN. IT LOOKS JUST AS A DOCUMENT WRITTEN OVER A HUNDRED YEARS AGO SHOULD LOOK!

WE KNOW HOFMANN COULD HAVE BEEN PRODUCING FORGERIES. HOW DO WE TELL WHICH ONES?

FLYNN DECIDED TO LOOK AT ONE OF THE HOFMANN DOCUMENTS UNDER ULTRAVIOLET LIGHT.

HEY, GEORGE, COME AND TAKE A LOOK AT THIS.

THE INK'S SURFACE IS CRACKED. IT LOOKS LIKE ALLIGATOR'S SKIN.

I THINK THE RAPID AGING AFFECTED THE GUM ARABIC IN THE INK, CAUSING THE WRINKLING. WE MAY HAVE FOUND A WAY OF SPOTTING THE FAKES.

THE WRINKLING WAS ONLY SEEN ON THOSE DOCUMENTS THAT HOFMANN HAD HANDLED. NOW THE POLICE COULD PROVE THAT HOFMANN WAS A FORGER AND HAD A MOTIVE FOR THE MURDERS.

WE FOUND OUT THAT THE MORMONS HAD ALREADY GIVEN HOFMANN ONE-HUNDRED-AND-EIGHTY-FIVE THOUSAND DOLLARS FOR THE McCLELLIN COLLECTION.

NOW THEY WANTED THE LETTERS OR THEIR MONEY BACK. BUT HOFMANN NEVER HAD THE COLLECTION TO SELL.

HE WAS GOING TO FORGE IT. TO DO THAT HE NEEDED MORE TIME. THAT'S WHY STEVEN CHRISTENSEN WAS MURDERED.

THE SECOND BOMB WAS MEANT TO THROW US OFF THE SCENT. IT DIDN'T MATTER WHO IT KILLED, AS LONG AS WE THOUGHT IT HAD SOMETHING TO DO WITH SHEETS'S FAILED BUSINESS.

WE DON'T KNOW WHO THE THIRD BOMB WAS MEANT FOR—CHRISTENSEN'S REPLACEMENT, MAYBE. HOFMANN PROBABLY BLEW HIMSELF UP BY ACCIDENT.

FACED WITH ALL THE EVIDENCE AGAINST HIM, HOFMANN PLEADED GUILTY TO SECOND-DEGREE MURDER AND GAVE A FULL CONFESSION. IN JANUARY 1987 HOFMANN WAS SENTENCED TO LIFE IN PRISON.

THE END

SAWBONES

DR. STEVEN SYMES STUDIED THE BONE SAMPLE. IT WAS PART OF A COLLECTION OF BONES THAT THE MEDICAL EXAMINER IN MINNEAPOLIS HAD SENT TO HIM. ALL THE BONES WERE FROM A DISMEMBERMENT CASE THE MEDICAL EXAMINER WAS TRYING TO SOLVE.

DR. SYMES WAS A FORENSIC ANTHROPOLOGIST AT MERCYHURST COLLEGE, ERIE, PENNSYLVANIA. HIS SPECIALTY WAS TOOLMARK ANALYSIS.

TOOLMARK ANALYSTS LOOK AT THE UNIQUE FEATURES OF CRIME SCENE OBJECTS, SUCH AS TIRE MARKS, SHOE PRINTS, AND BULLETS. DR. SYMES WAS INTERESTED IN THE MARKS THAT SHARP-BLADED TOOLS LEAVE ON BONES AND WHAT THEY CAN TELL. THE TOOLMARK ANALYSIS OF BONES IS A NEW SCIENCE, HOWEVER.

IT WAS 1987 AND DR. SYMES HAD JUST STARTED A NEW JOB IN NASHVILLE, TENNESSEE. HE WAS WORKING AS THE FORENSIC ANTHROPOLOGIST IN THE MEDICAL EXAMINER'S OFFICE WHEN...

THE DETECTIVE WAS RIGHT. DR. SYMES WAS THE "BONE DOC" AND SHOULD KNOW. BUT NO RESEARCH HAD BEEN DONE ON HOW SAWS CUT THROUGH BONE.

HEY, DOC, I DON'T SUPPOSE YOU COULD TELL ME WHAT MADE THESE MARKS ON THIS ARM BONE?

IT LOOKS TO ME LIKE IT WAS A SAW, DETECTIVE..

I CAN SEE THAT, BUT WHAT **KIND** OF SAW? YOU'RE THE BONE DOC. YOU SHOULD KNOW.

DR. SYMES DECIDED TO DO THE RESEARCH HIMSELF.

HE STARTED BY BORROWING AND BUYING EVERY TYPE OF KNIFE AND SAW HE COULD.

HE USED HAND TOOLS AND POWER TOOLS.

OVER THE NEXT TWENTY YEARS, WHENEVER HE HAD THE TIME, DR. SYMES USED MANY DIFFERENT SAWS AND KNIVES TO CUT THROUGH PIECES OF BONE.

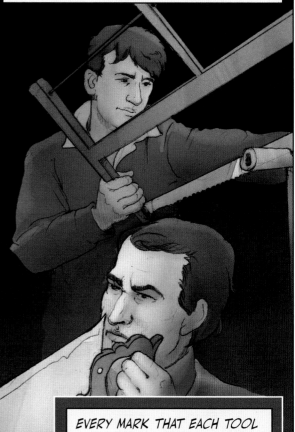

EVERY MARK THAT EACH TOOL MADE WAS EXAMINED. HE WAS TRYING TO MATCH A TYPE OF TOOL WITH A TYPE OF MARK.

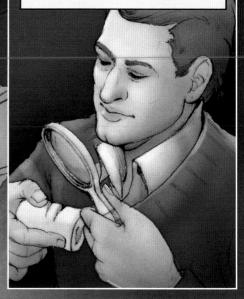

DR. SYMES BEGAN TO EXAMINE THE BONES THAT HE HAD BEEN SENT. HE NOTICED FROM THE SHAPE OF THE KERF* THAT THE CUTS HAD BEEN MADE BY A SAW.

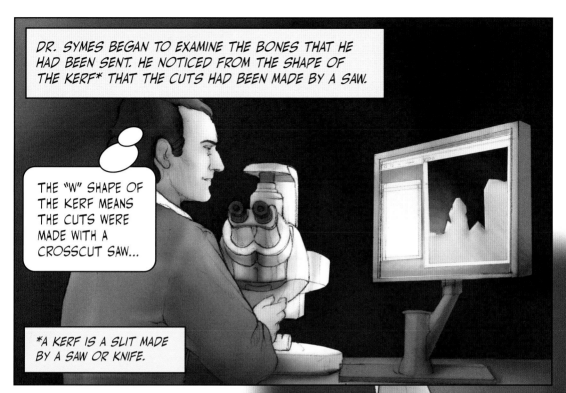

THE "W" SHAPE OF THE KERF MEANS THE CUTS WERE MADE WITH A CROSSCUT SAW...

*A KERF IS A SLIT MADE BY A SAW OR KNIFE.

...SO IT WASN'T A POWER SAW—THEY HAVE RIPSAW, NOT CROSSCUT, BLADES.

THE TEETH OF CROSSCUT SAWS ARE SHAPED LIKE SMALL KNIVES AND BENT LEFT AND RIGHT ALONG THE SAW BLADE, LEAVING A "VALLEY" DOWN THE MIDDLE.

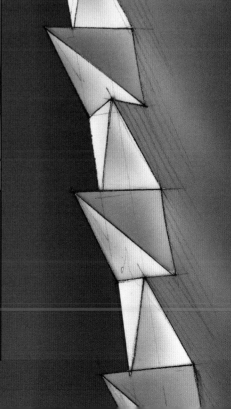

DR. SYMES MEASURED THE WIDTH OF THE KERF AT 0.05 INCHES (1.27 MILLIMETERS).

BOW SAWS HAVE CROSSCUT BLADES, TOO, BUT THEY'RE THINNER. SO THAT RULES THEM OUT.

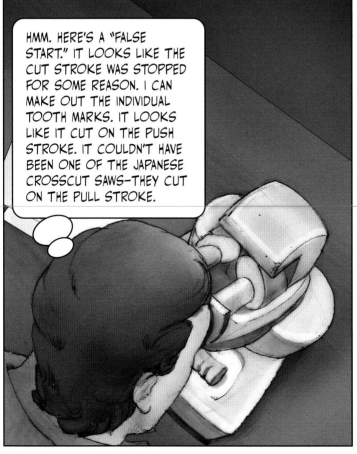

HMM. HERE'S A "FALSE START." IT LOOKS LIKE THE CUT STROKE WAS STOPPED FOR SOME REASON. I CAN MAKE OUT THE INDIVIDUAL TOOTH MARKS. IT LOOKS LIKE IT CUT ON THE PUSH STROKE. IT COULDN'T HAVE BEEN ONE OF THE JAPANESE CROSSCUT SAWS—THEY CUT ON THE PULL STROKE.

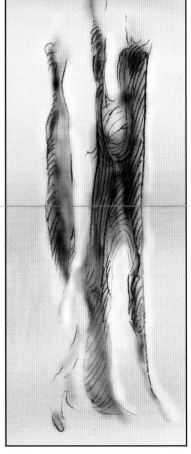

BY MEASURING THE DISTANCE BETWEEN THE TOOTH MARKS DR. SYMES COULD WORK OUT THE TPI* OF THE SAW. IT ALSO TOLD HIM IN WHICH DIRECTION THE CUT WAS MADE.

NINE TPI—THAT MAKES IT TOO BIG TO BE A BACKSAW. IT WAS PROBABLY ONE OF THE SMALLER CARPENTER'S SAWS.

*TEETH PER INCH.

THEN, AMONG THE SAW CUTS, DR. SYMES SPOTTED A DIFFERENT KIND OF CUT.

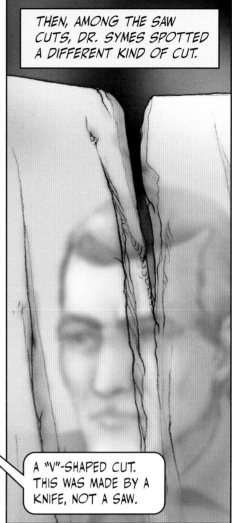

A "V"-SHAPED CUT. THIS WAS MADE BY A KNIFE, NOT A SAW.

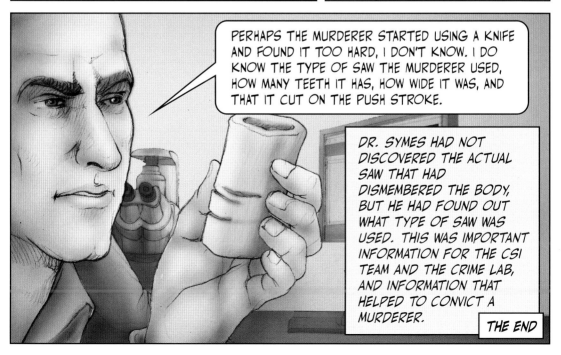

PERHAPS THE MURDERER STARTED USING A KNIFE AND FOUND IT TOO HARD, I DON'T KNOW. I DO KNOW THE TYPE OF SAW THE MURDERER USED, HOW MANY TEETH IT HAS, HOW WIDE IT WAS, AND THAT IT CUT ON THE PUSH STROKE.

DR. SYMES HAD NOT DISCOVERED THE ACTUAL SAW THAT HAD DISMEMBERED THE BODY, BUT HE HAD FOUND OUT WHAT TYPE OF SAW WAS USED. THIS WAS IMPORTANT INFORMATION FOR THE CSI TEAM AND THE CRIME LAB, AND INFORMATION THAT HELPED TO CONVICT A MURDERER.

THE END

AN AUTOPSY WAS CARRIED OUT BY DR. BARBARA CHAITIN.

THE BODY'S FEMALE. IT'S BADLY DECOMPOSED. SHE MUST HAVE BEEN IN THE WATER FOR QUITE SOME TIME.

THE HIP HASN'T FULLY FUSED TOGETHER, SO I'D SAY SHE WAS BETWEEN TWENTY AND TWENTY-TWO YEARS OLD.

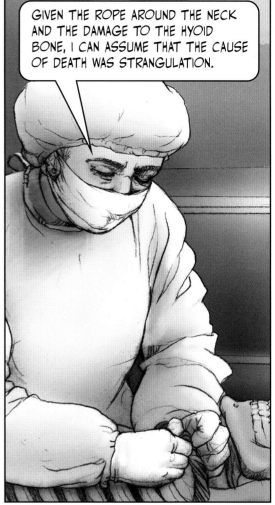

GIVEN THE ROPE AROUND THE NECK AND THE DAMAGE TO THE HYOID BONE, I CAN ASSUME THAT THE CAUSE OF DEATH WAS STRANGULATION.

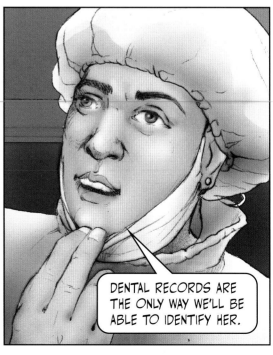

DENTAL RECORDS ARE THE ONLY WAY WE'LL BE ABLE TO IDENTIFY HER.

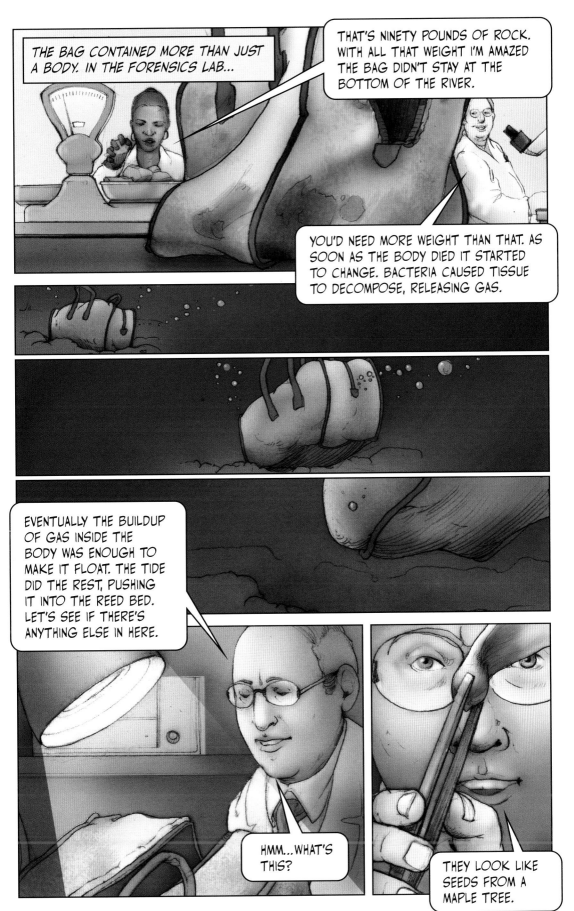

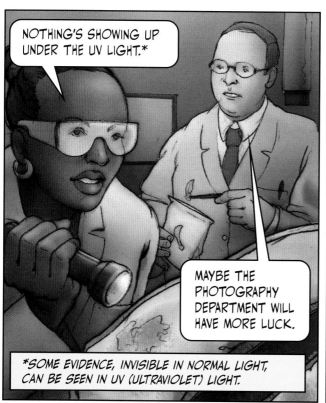

NOTHING'S SHOWING UP UNDER THE UV LIGHT.*

MAYBE THE PHOTOGRAPHY DEPARTMENT WILL HAVE MORE LUCK.

*SOME EVIDENCE, INVISIBLE IN NORMAL LIGHT, CAN BE SEEN IN UV (ULTRAVIOLET) LIGHT.

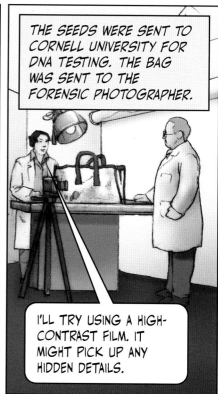

THE SEEDS WERE SENT TO CORNELL UNIVERSITY FOR DNA TESTING. THE BAG WAS SENT TO THE FORENSIC PHOTOGRAPHER.

I'LL TRY USING A HIGH-CONTRAST FILM. IT MIGHT PICK UP ANY HIDDEN DETAILS.

LATER.

LOOK AT THESE. THEY'RE PRINTS OF THE BAG.

THEY SHOW MARKS ON THE BOTTOM OF THE BAG. IT HAD BEEN SITTING ON SOMETHING WITH A DISTINCTIVE PATTERN.

AT LAST DENTAL RECORDS PROVIDED THE POLICE WITH A NAME. SHE WAS 21-YEAR-OLD MARY ANN POWELL FROM HALFMOON, NEW YORK.

THE SHERIFF'S OFFICE, SARATOGA, NEW YORK.

SHE WAS REPORTED MISSING IN OCTOBER 1994, BY HER HUSBAND, WARREN POWELL. AT THE MOMENT HE'S IN JAIL ON A DRUGS CHARGE.

I THINK WE SHOULD TAKE A LOOK AT POWELL'S HOME.

MISSING

POWELL'S HOME IN HALFMOON...

POWELL'S PLACE IS OVER THERE BY THAT MAPLE TREE.

WEREN'T THERE MAPLE SEEDS IN THE SPORTS BAG THEY FOUND?

I'LL LET FORENSICS KNOW.

IS THIS POWELL'S BOAT?

SO THE NEIGHBORS SAY.

I THINK FORENSICS WILL WANT TO LOOK AT IT.

SAMPLES FROM THE TREE WERE COLLECTED, AND THE BOAT WAS TAKEN TO THE LAB.

THESE SLATS ON THE BOAT SEAT GIVE ME AN IDEA.

ON THE LEFT IS THE PHOTOGRAPH OF THE MARKS ON THE BAG BOTTOM.

AND HERE IS A PHOTOGRAPH OF THE BOAT SEAT.

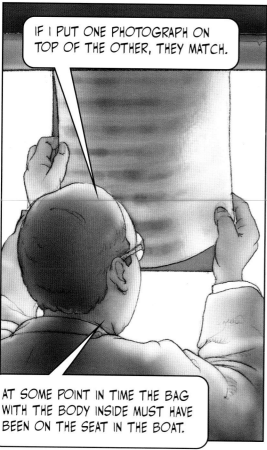

IF I PUT ONE PHOTOGRAPH ON TOP OF THE OTHER, THEY MATCH.

AT SOME POINT IN TIME THE BAG WITH THE BODY INSIDE MUST HAVE BEEN ON THE SEAT IN THE BOAT.

CORNELL UNIVERSITY SENT THE TEST RESULTS FROM THE SEED AND FROM THE TREE SAMPLES...

THE SEEDS TAKEN FROM THE BAG CAME FROM THE TREE NEXT TO POWELL'S HOME. THEIR DNA IS THE SAME.

SO WE CAN LINK THE BAG AND THE BODY TO POWELL'S BOAT **AND** TO HIS HOME.

EVENTUALLY THE POLICE MANAGED TO PIECE TOGETHER WHAT HAD HAPPENED. ON OCTOBER 1, 1994, THE POWELLS HAD BEEN ARGUING. THIS ARGUMENT ENDED IN MURDER.

WARREN POWELL HAD TO THINK FAST. HE WENT OUT AND BOUGHT A BOAT AND A LARGE HOCKEY KIT BAG.

HE PUT THE BODY INTO THE BAG.

UNDERNEATH THE MAPLE TREE...

...POWELL WEIGHTED THE BAG...

...AND TOOK IT TO COLUMBIA COUNTY, NEW YORK.

POWELL KNEW THIS STRETCH OF THE HUDSON RIVER. IT WAS WHERE HE HAD GROWN UP.

WHEN WARREN POWELL PUSHED THE BAG INTO THE HUDSON, HE DID NOT KNOW THERE WERE MAPLE SEEDS IN IT.

NEITHER DID HE REALIZE THAT MARKS ON THE BOTTOM OF THE BAG WOULD BE TRACED BACK TO HIS BOAT.

IN 1997 POWELL WAS FOUND GUILTY OF MURDERING HIS WIFE, MARY ANN, AND WAS SENTENCED TO SPEND AT LEAST 25 YEARS IN PRISON.

THE END

OTHER FAMOUS CASES

Here are some more celebrated cases that feature crime scene investigation and forensic science.

DEADLY INSURANCE

On November 1, 1955, a United Airlines passenger plane crashed into a Colorado beet field, killing all 44 people on board. The wreckage was spread too wide for a mechanical fault to have caused it. The plane must have exploded in flight. The FBI was called in. The plane was reassembled from all the pieces that could be collected. The investigators saw that a bomb had been planted in someone's luggage. The FBI found out that several life insurance policies had been taken out on behalf of Daisie King, a victim. They were traced back to Jack Graham, her son. He eventually confessed to planting the bomb in his mother's suitcase.

GUM'S THE WORD

Walter Childs had been shot in the head and stabbed many times. The only piece of evidence that the CSI officers could find was a single wad of gum stuck to a dresser. The blob of gum was sent to forensic dentist Dr. Norman Sperber. He made a mold of the gum and a mold of the teeth of Patricia Beibe, who was a suspect. She claimed not to have known Childs, but the gum fitted one of Beibe's teeth perfectly. She later confessed to the murder.

DRAINPIPE OF DEATH

Thirty-year-old stab victim Belinda Wood managed to call the operator before dying. When the police arrived at the murder scene they could only stay a few minutes—someone had started a fire and the whole building was ablaze. Donald Catching, who lived in an apartment beneath Belinda Wood's, was arrested on suspicion of the murder, but all the evidence had been destroyed, so it would be difficult to prove. The medical examiner, Dr. Burton, had an idea. He managed to climb from Catching's apartment up to Wood's apartment

using a drainpipe. Dr. Burton's arms were scratched and bruised, and there were friction burns from the climb. They were exactly the same as the injuries that were found on Catching's arms when he was arrested. They helped to convict him of Wood's murder.

KISS AND TELL

After a woman had robbed a small Californian bank, she walked toward the exit and straight into the bank's glass door. She was stunned for a moment but still managed to escape. The robber left no evidence behind, except for a lipstick print on the glass door. But without a lip print database it could not be matched to anyone. Then, after a tip-off, the police were given a name, Jonathan Jackson. Even though Jackson was a man, the police arrested him. His lip print perfectly matched the one on the bank door. Jackson had tried to fool everyone by disguising himself as a woman.

POLICE DO NOT CROSS

GLOSSARY

analyzed A subject that has been carefully examined.

antique An object that is collected because it is old.

archives The place where past documents and records are stored.

authenticated To have shown something to be genuine.

challenge A test of ability.

conclusions Decisions arrived at using reasoning.

coroner A court official who investigates murders and violent deaths.

culprit A person who has committed a crime.

database A collection of related facts.

deduced To have come to an answer by using a thought process based on reason.

detonation An explosion.

detonator A small device used to set off a larger explosion.

distinctive A special quality that can single a thing or person out.

DNA Deoxyribonucleic acid, a material that can duplicate itself and is found in every organic cell.

entomologist A person who studies insects.

finance The business of managing money.

galls Round growths on the stem or leaf of a plant.

hyoid A small bone in the throat.

igniter A small device that starts the burning of a fuel.

investor A person who puts money into a business.

logical Something that is reasoned.

mercury A metal that conducts electricity and is a liquid at room temperature.

motives The reasons behind someone's actions.

snagged To become caught on something that juts out.

suburbs The neighborhoods that surround a city or large town.

ultraviolet (UV) That part of the spectrum that comes after violet light and is invisible.

unique A feature or quality that can be found in one place and nowhere else.

vaporized A substance that has been changed into a gas.

warrant A legal document that allows court officials to carry out individual court orders.

FOR MORE INFORMATION

ORGANIZATIONS

International High Technology Crime Investigation Association
HTCIA, Inc.
4021 Woodcreek Oaks Blvd., Ste. 156, #209
Roseville, CA 95747
(916) 408-1751
Web site: http://www.htcia.org

International Association for Identification
2535 Pilot Knob Road, Suite 117
Mendota Heights, MN 55120-1120
(651) 681-8566
Web site: http://www.theiai.org

FOR FURTHER READING

Campbell, Andrea. *Forensic Science: Evidence, Clues, and Investigation.* New York, NY: Chelsea House Publishers, 1999.

Dahl, Michael. *Poison Evidence.* Mankato, MN: Capstone Press, 2004.

Fridell, Ron. *Forensic Science.* Minneapolis, MN: Lerner Publications, 2007.

Rollins, Barbara, B and Michael Dahl. *Fingerprint Evidence.* Mankato, MN: Capstone Press, 2004.

Webber, Diane. *Shot and Framed: Photographers at the Crime Scene* (24/7 Science Behind the Scenes: Forensic Files). London, England: Franklin Watts, 2007.

INDEX

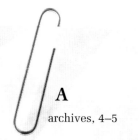

Web Sites

Due to the changing nature of Internet links, Rosen Publishing has developed an online list of Web sites related to the subject of this book. This site is updated regularly. Please use this link to access the list:

http://www.rosenlinks.com/gfs/csin